Conversations

with

Idras

Celebrity Lies Hand-Picked for You

A work of satire

Written by ZZ Claybourne

WITH BONUS BLANK DOODLING PAGES

Illustrated by Patty Templeton

CONVERSATIONS WITH IDRAS

Copyright 2020 by Clarence Young

This is a work of satire. Names, persons, and events portrayed in this book are products of the author's imagination and are used entirely fictitiously.

Obsidian Sky Books
Detroit, MI

www.obsidianskybooks.com

ISBN 978-1-7322980-2-6 (trade paperback)

First Edition: December 2020

Cover art by Brett Massé

Introduction

Pretty sure you've figured out who that's supposed to be on the cover, eh? Only thing is, it's *not* supposed to be him. I don't know him. Don't know a thing about what keeps him up at night, what drives him to connect with others, or what kind of speech he'd make at holiday dinner. I don't know any of the fine folks mentioned in this papery attempt to briefly pull you away from the trashfire in the foyer. But I know I have this very cool image of one of them in my mind: a confidante, a foil, someone who's had a look beneath the world's undercarriage and knows the knickers aren't entirely posh.

The friend in this book is the invisible mate we all need. A James Bond thespian DJ with a sharp eye and a ready laugh. I got nothing but respect for the real deal. We're not making fun here. This's just a fire extinguisher, and I'm here to help you take aim.

So let's get jiggy with it.

"You need to know"—sips Cognac from eclectic beaker—"a few things. First: that I don't know Idras Melba; this Buccololly couch (made-up designer name) is yak leather; our economic systems are bullshit but so is the last season of *Game of Thrones* and we live with that; Gin Paltrow's never unfriended me but I did have dinner with Pam Dear. And far as I know, Viola Mavis isn't psychic."

Stares at you in urbane disaffection. Waits till you're just about to speak to interrupt you by taking another sip.

"Now, if you'd like to continue this session, sit back and prepare to be lied to."

Everything is fine.

Idras Melba Is Cooler Than Me

See, this one time me and Idras are walking down the street. Totally true story that never happened. And he starts ribbing me, right, going "Bruv", "Bruv", "Bruv" just to piss me off but it's not working 'cause we're on our way to deliver a couch to a needy family. Family's rich as fuk, just needed a couch. Lived a block away from Idras, so we're like, we'll just carry it. Idras had 7 couches in his damn house, just in his living room. "Idras, why you got so many couches?" That's when he starts bruvving me. "If you weren't so piss poor," goes he, "you'd know every couch has a dif function, a'right? Elevate y'self, fam. Elevate." Fuck you, Idras Melba.

We're taking the couch to Viola Mavis's house. Good people, Viola; gives you cheese grits whenever you come by. I love cheese grits. But all I'm hearing is "Bruv."

"I'ma kick you in the nuts, Idras Melba."

"That's how you're playing this, fam? You wanna row here on the street? Gonna have a go? Tickling me nibblies? Touching things lightly?"

"What?

"Just sayin', bruv, aim higher, hey? Writing that weird wonk all'a time."

"Shut the fuck up, Idras Melba."

"Never gonna get more couches in your life, fam."

"CARRY THE DAMN COUCH, IDRAS MELBA."

It's at this particular point that Viola sees us coming. "Idras fucking with you?" she says.

"Yes!"

"Carry the damn couch, Idras!" she snaps. I immediately know he ain't getting no cheese in his grits. Inwardly, I am pleased.

Idras sets the couch down. "Alice..."

"You know damn well that's not my name."

"Alice?"

"Don't—"

"What have you done?" he finishes.

Dude's in the zone. I set my end down and sit on the couch.

"Every single time..." mutters Viola.

"It didn't have to play like this," he's saying. "I just wanted bruv—"

I tip a finger at Viola.

"—to apply himself, y'know, get him more than one

sofa his entire damn life. He's capable of 2 sofas easily. Lookit 'im there, his one-couch ass."

"Oi!" I shout, and that's all the London gibberish I can come up with. They look at me like I'm crazy. I let 'em have that one.

Now, it's been raining a bit, right? It's not muddy but me feet are wet. And it's a cream couch. So of course I'm thinking to Rick James it, 'cause seriously, I coulda still been home with my Rosario Dawdur coloring book just as happy as all shit.

"Mate's writing shit about whales 'n demon babies 'n Smurfs. Barbarian Smurfs, Alice; you know what that is?! Do you? Alice?"

"Sweet historically-accurate dusky Jesus," Viola mutters.

Then, simple as everything, Idras reaches under a cushion and pulls out a grey overcoat. You know the one.

"The fuck…" says Viola.

"Idras, we ain't gotta do this," I say. "Don't put on the coat, man."

He's got an arm in. He's looking me dead in the eye. He's moving the other arm into position.

"Nothing but pain down that road, my dude," I implore.

"I loved you, bruv! Like a bruvver…"

"There's a T in that word," says Viola.

Other arm goes in.

He's at full Luther.

Only one thing I can think to end this. Fast, I draw my feet onto the couch. I see his eyes go wide but it's too late.

"FUCK YO COUCH, IDRAS MELBA!"

And it's Full Rick James on that baby-ass idolatry.

"I am not ever writing *The Fast and The Furious: The Next Generation*! I got 2 ass cheeks; they can't sit on 7 couches at once! FUCK YO COUCH, IDRAS." My dirty boots are wailing away, baby-leather like oh, oh my, oh dear, oh no. Nooooo. Buccololly couch. Nooooo.

"Fuck. Yo. Buccololly. Couch."

At this point I know ain't neither one of us getting any cheese grits.

I reach under a cushion, pull out a book. Pro-tip: Always hide a stash.

It's *The Brothers Jetstream*. I wrote it. It's got a giant psychic whale in it. Idras has never read it. I'm about to swak him right in the face with it when Viola does a twist: she quotes from it. Stops us both dead on.

"He moved in the direction of the Atlantidean capital.

Nobody knew about the presence of vampires in Atlantis, bloodletting little ticks. It was up to him to make sure it remained that way, since, by the time he was done, they would every last one of them have been quietly bested."

She quoted it as fuckin Viola Mavis, so it sounded sweet and fraught and oh fuk sumbody 'bout to get fooooked up as only Viola Mavis can, like, you might think you got an A in crazy but don't test me, this is my natural-ass hair.

My mouth drops. "Viola Mavis... you read that book?"

"Course not. I read your mind. How you think I know you always want cheese grits?"

Viola Mavis...is motherfucking psychic.

A gigantic psychic Viola Mavis. Next book is fucking written.

Idras breaks the joy. "Where d'we go from here? Oi? Stalemate as I see it, 'cuz you want a couch, you want obscurity, I'm not lettin' anybody get 'urt here, right, so—"

"Idras, I'll buy another couch," I say.

"OK then. Right." He sniffs, looks about. "Let's get this cleaned up, let's get this moved. Viola, you all right with that?"

"I just wanted a sofa for my cat."

"Fam, fam, it's good right?" He's looking at us and

nodding. "It's good."

But I'm very quietly but kinda definitely thinking to myself, fuck yo couch, Idras Melba, all in lower case while I'm picking up my end of the sofa again, not looking at Viola Mavis at all 'cause, y'know, I know she's in my head.

Viola Mavis is in my head, fam.

Next book is fucking written.

SHUT YOUR HOLE, ANAL ITCH.

The Classics

So Joyce Hall O'Oates calls me up drunk one night. Totally fucken true story except it never happened. "Hell you doin, you punk ass beeyotch?" she slurs, and I'm all, "Joyce, the order says you can't do this anymore," and she literally SCREAMS, "SHUT YOUR HOLE, ANAL ITCH," then launches into, "I'm gonna write something filthy, I'm gonna write something filthy make your ass cry, c'mon, do it, write something filthy."

"I don't wanna write something filthy with you, Joyce!"

"WRITE SUMTHIN FILTHYYYY," and she slams the phone down thinking it's an old-style handset but calls me back saying she broke her phone. "Buy me new phone, you punk ass bee—"

"Joyce."

"What?"

"Joyce."

"What?"

"Joyce."

"I'ma cut your ass."

"If I write something filthy will you stop calling me?"

"Who the hell are you?"

"Joyce."

"Who the hell are you? Oh shit, I'm falling," and I hear tumbling, a clatter. Silence.

"You OK?"

"I fell."

"I'll write something filthy."

"Know what, Jonathan? I love you."

"I'm not Jonathan Fronzen, Joyce. We're not doing this again."

"JONATHAN FRONZEN, I'MA PEE IN YOUR SHOE WHEN I SEE YOU. I'ma be like, 'Jonathan Fronzen, thas a nice shoe,' and you'll be like, 'Thanks,' and I'll be, 'Take off one,' and you'll be, 'Huh?' and I'ma nod at your left shoe. 'Take that off,' and, 'I'm fukken Joyce Hall O'Oates, you're gonna take off your fukken shoe,' and I'm gonna be like, 'HAAAAAA WHIZ!' then run."

Then she starts crying. "I don't pee in people's shoes, guy on phone!"

"I know, Joyce."

"I'm a nice ladee."

"Utmost respect, Joyce."

"Jennifuh Lopez heard somebody call me J-CO then she stole it."

"Hard world, Joyce."

"Hard world. You gonna write?"

"Yeah, I'm gonna write."

"Ok, call you tomorrow."

And that's how *It's Turning Purple, I Think We Should Quit* came to be.

Amazod ebook only.

Idras's Long-Ass Speech

Noticed 3 things right off: Viola wouldn't let go of the knife, Idras had sweet potato pie crust crumbs on his sweater, and the lady who'd played Alice on "Luther" looked increasingly uncomfortable, but Idras was in the zone, giving what so far had been a ten-minute pre-dinner speech in his London flat.

"Idras," I say, having gotten his attention during a lull. "'Sposed to be a blessing, brother. United Nations, not so much." Between us were yams, some vindaloo, candied swine, stuffing made with imported White Castle burgers 'cause, y'know, Idras ("Imported makes shit artisanal, fam!"), jollof rice, cabbage—

Idras was keeping me from garlic motherloving shrimp.

Viola Mavis was hungry. And not wearing one of her good wigs. Which meant she'd rushed out. Shit was going to turn into the veritable show soon.

And poor, gorgeous, honeydew-lipped Ms. Duluth Wilson (who, also, unfortunately, was in the Johnny Derp *Lone Ranger* movie, which was why I figured she felt so unrelentingly uncomfortable, having that over her head and all), she probably wanted in her heart of hearts to spend a day with her family and not rehashing the Thanksgiving Ides of March colonial-style. Nobody'd called me a traitorous bastard yet in England but it was coming. But Idras was all, "I want my best fam to spend Thanksgiving wi' me…in my flat…my table…London. London." And he'd asked for my mama's sweet potato pie recipe. "Gonna make sure you eat so much pie you can't speak, bruv!" he'd said, getting more excited as he talked. "Gettin' that mouth on my pie, bruv!"

Sometimes it's best just to pack a bag, let TSA get their jollies off, and fly to London to have dinner at Idras Melba's house rather than put up a fight.

"Did I fly you out here, bruv?" he says to my gentle admonition. "You want me nailing my hand to this table so you'll pay attention, that it? That what you need for a bit of patience?"

"I'm just sayin', bruh…"

Viola Mavis has not put the knife down.

"You rushing the evening?" he says. "Huh? You feeling that orgy later with Alice?"

"What?" says Ms. Wilson.

Viola slams the knife point into the table. "I told you I wasn't doing an orgy with you!"

"THERE'S NOT GONNA BE AN ORGY!" I bellow. You'd think I could get through at least one holiday minus that. "Idras, wrap this the fuck up."

"I haven't even gotten to where I speak Italian."

"I plan to kick you so hard in the nuts," Viola mumbles.

"Here's what we're gonna do, Idras: I'm gonna take over the saying of grace, then you get to cap it, cut up some ceremonial meat, and step back to avoid catching hands and knives. Let go of the knife, Viola," I say.

"No."

I glance at Ms. Wilson. I wonder if she's ever kissed anybody and they flat out fainted? I hope I'm not licking my lips when I glance at her. Am I glancing too much? That why she feel uncomfortable? Not enough? She's probably used to lots of recognition. I lick my lips. Stupid ass Lone Ranger movie. I put on a reassuring voice, a Mr. Rogers smile. "There won't be an orgy, Ms. Wilson."

"I'm not even sure why I'm here," she says.

"Bruv, what's this thing with you and orgies?" Idras asks, suddenly full of concern for me like he's not the one who pulled it out of his ass in the first place. "You fly out here to touch my butt? You feelin' nibbly for me?"

"I'm not here for your butt, Idras."

"You want a go on Thanksgiving, is that it?"

"I just wanna eat, bruh."

"Leave that Tr*mp family reunion shit at the door, huh. We're fam."

I stand, tired of waiting for my jollof rice! Viola's grip tightens on the knife hilt. Ms. Wilson, who's kept a small, tasteful bag in her lap the whole evening, slowly reaches inside it...

"Look," I say, looking at each face. "I'm thankful for each and every one of you. Idras, you fuckin' keep me on my toes. Viola. I'm truly sorry for your couch."

"Fuck you."

"Blessings, all blessings. Duluth, you can freshen up your lipstick before we eat if you want."

"Fam, you're embarrassing yourself," Idras interjects.

I sigh. My stomach grumbles. I run a hand down my face. "Quick, honest, and gracious, that's me, and Idras, I swear to god if you say that's what she said..." But he doesn't. I think he feels where I'm going with this. "We're all a mess," I say, "except for you, Ms. Wilson. Duluth."

"Alice," says Idras.

"But are we intentional messes? We're not deliberate asses. Idras here isn't keeping us from the food because he's a dick, he's doing it because he loves us. That long ass speech included digressions about forced labor versus permaculture gardening because this man's heart is huge, yeah? And look at this table. Does it not scream for not only wealth redistribution but wealth redefinition?! That knife in your hand costs more than I make in a week, Viola. This food, which by the way—" I do chef's kiss at Melba— "would give Bacchus boner shame. The aluminum foil in all our purses and bags is going to be well-used, yet I think we're giving thanks for more than that, right? We have to be thankful that we make connections as humans before anything else, because, because all that is good flows from that inception point."

Idras, at some point, had pulled up the Captain Kirk speech music on his phone.

"It is a given…" I punctuate with the thumb-fist, "that we will reach a point where gain and production are no longer prevailing gods…that we will see the brilliant humanity in each other over the imaginary profits…that when we sit down to say thanks we are saying thank you for what you, you, Viola Mavis, you, Idras Melba, you, Duluth Wilson of the gawds…have brought to my ineffable life. Are we enriching each other in what matters? That, my friends, is the question we must find an answer to give thanks for." Idras cranks the volume to a timely swell. "Do I hear a no vote?"

The room is silent of voices a moment.

Idras turns off the phone. "Fam," he says. "In every revolution—" He picks up the carving knife. "—there's shutting up and eating the bird." The warmth of his smile is real. "I gotta confess: I had pie earlier. Loads of it. And here I am making you wait…"

"It's all right, bruv," I say.

His eyes are watering up. He accedes that it's past time for all to eat. He cuts the bird. He passes it down.

I come around and give him a big hug.

Viola keeps hold of the knife, but fukkit, it's an Idras Melba Thanksgiving.

Blatant Lies in the Enema's Bounty Store

Gin Paltrow kept asking what I thought about a Pepper Potts standalone, which of course I'm hell no, but out of the corner of my eye I see the ghost of David Bowie writing on the wind in bright blue fog, "We could be heroes…" but I'm still noooooope. But to deny Gin Paltrow is to anger Gin Paltrow.

She takes a swipe. I easily evade. A baby yawning would connect harder. Then she throws unused, empty syringes at me. They smell vaguely of moose placenta. Trust that. Very not cool. Just as I'm about to pick her up between my fingers I hear Idras come up behind me; he doesn't make noise but you can hear his walk.

My first thought: If he brings up that damn couch…

"Bruv, she throwing needles at you?"

"I know this, Idras!"

He shakes his head. "You've lost control of your destiny, man. You're adrift. Kind of fucked up, innit?"

"Idras, what the hell are you talking about?"

"You're adrift."

So I fucking ignore him totally because Gin is shaking a bottle of lactose-free milk to skeet me.

"Don't skeet me, Gin." This is precisely why I don't hang around celebrities.

"Pepper Potts is the center of the MCU," says Gin.

"When's the last time you had a meal, darlin'?" I ask.

("Bruv? ...Bruv? Ask her why she's carrying syringes. Adrift as fuck, that is.")

("Shut the fuck up, Idras.")

"All I want is to be seen," Gin says. She drops her arms but doesn't let the milk go. She looks me in the eye for the first time since cutting in line at the naturopath's. Let no one impugn your tumeric root extract. Ever.

"I know," I say, voice level, calm, because a new-age starlet on edge is a bomb of such prickly proportions you can't even if it should.

"I want to be loved," she says.

"No one will love you if you do that movie, Gin. They'll shun you. Don't be shunned. Give me the milk."

"Just—FUCK!"

"Give me the milk, Gin."

("Fucking adrift," says Idras. "Y'know, when we moved that couch I told you, I told you," and he waggles his finger dramatically because apparently it's what he told me.)

"I wore the suit in Iron Man 3," says she.

"I know. That movie sucked."

"Head in a box," she murmurs, then repeats it over and over. Gin's gone.

Endgame. I gotta go for the milk.

"Alice!" says Idras, drawing the word out till it's a paragraph of text and subtext.

"Don't call her that, Idras…"

"Aaalice…don't do it."

"You're out of your element, Idras!" I snap. Too late. Gin's looking dead at him. I've seen that look before. It's the look of an actress about to go beneath a Kardashian on the cover of *People*.

She shakes the milk furiously.

She pops the top.

It squirts up Idras's nose.

He goes down. He's gagging and flailing, totally adrift. Totally vulnerable.

I gotta stop this.

"Pepper…I'll always love you."

She freezes.

"It's always been you," I say. "I wasn't smart enough to know it but—"

"But now it's too late."

"Yes."

("Fucking adrift! Shit!")

"Let me hug you, Gin. Let me hug you like you've never been hugged, for the first time in your life, come and receive abundance."

I open my arms to her. I got nothing to hide, nothing to gain, nothing to lose. We gotta get out of this line one way or another. It's only a matter of time before the cashier sneers and embarrasses us by opening another line.

She won't remember the hug. We're gonna leave this store, go our separate ways, never see each other again. I don't consider it a waste though. She's not throwing needles. The milk carton's useless in her hands unless she spills it. Gin Paltrow is sighing against my chest and relaxing for probably the first time in her life. She's not even Gin Paltrow at that moment, she's just somebody letting herself be held.

Human.

Very human.

Endgame.

"I signed for a Heimdall prequel," says Idras.

Gin tightens.

Dammit.

I Never Krumped for My Father

Jody Whutley laughed at me that one time I tried to krump so I never tried it again, but something was telling me—as I watched Jared Feeto approach on that hi-rollin' Sunset Blvd street—that the show was about to begin. True enough, Feeto stopped right in the middle of me and Queen Maloofah talking about Preence laying absolute WASTE to mofos with his 1986 birthday concert in Detroit, traffic whizzing by, Hollywood slowly dying, AXE spray and imported perfume vying for lung space…and did not this ruby-lipped bastich break off a piece of disrespectful poplock that made Queen skeet out some of her drink?! Oh, it was on, best believe it was on. But I let it slow burn. Acted like he wasn't even there. He proceeds to crotch hop. Queen's eyes become slits but I'm like, be cool. Said that to her telepathically. Why? Because Queen's a level one telepath here to make sure Wendy Wollums never reaches true power. Then we're talking about the drum solo Preence did on "America" at that concert. Jared encircles us in a breakdance walk and drops, thinking he's going to intimidate us with shoulder roll leg copters.

Then he stands, huffing a little. Bead of sweat traveling down.

That's when I know I've got him. Rule #1: you don't sweat. Fool.

I pull my shirt halfway off—which rightfully startles him—and lunge right at him, stopping inches away balanced on the big toe of my left foot. I'm 'bout to krump the living fuck out of Jared Feeto, I feel it building...but ain't that Jody Whutley coming out of a ridiculously expensive (and misspelled) bodega across the street where you didn't buy water you bought Wutuhr: the Experience by Giovanni. I can't have Jody Whutley laugh at me twice.

Jared is still frozen, he doesn't know what to do, he wasn't expecting MY ENTIRE ASS TO KRUMP HIM back to boy band nineties. I'm still on that toe, shirt half off, body vibrating with the energy of 7 Magic Mikes. Queen sees Jody. Jody sees Queen. *I can mindwipe the whole thing from her memory* Queen says. *Do it* I say.

And then the shirt flies off.

All I'm gonna say is if you're wondering why Jared Feeto sits at bus stops shaking his head no all the time while scissoring the legs of a Barbie doll like she's a ballerina, ask him why he felt the need to step to a middle-aged writer with so many rejections that "nothing to lose" is not just an enticement it's a way of life. Ask him why he thought he could poplock in front of Queen Maloofah unasked and unannounced on that smoggy-assed Cali day.

Ask Jared Feeto has he seen my hairy belly krump and roll. When he says yes, track that tear till it hangs off his chin. Let him know you see it.

Then leave him there, cuz he got what he deserved.

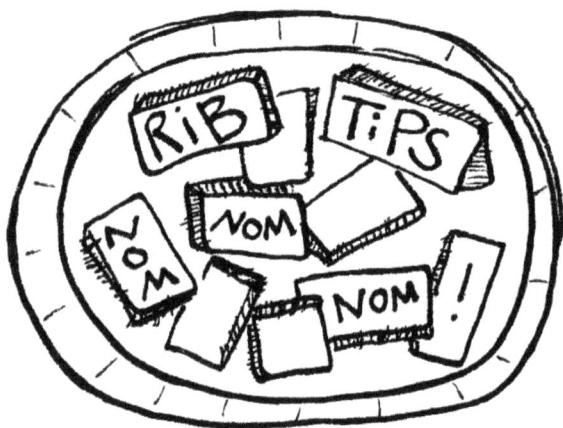

Desperation Rib Tips

It's been a long week, and I'm relaxing. Little jazz on, some half-ass desperation rib tips plated from a chain restaurant, onion straws on the side; just because you're relaxing doesn't mean the butt muscles shouldn't work out. Not feeling TV, not feeling Flix. What to read's on my mind. I'm thinking something light, some laughter—

"Bruv!"

DAMMIT, IDRAS. DAMMIT, DAMMIT, DAMMIT.

"Bruv...I think I broke it."

I refuse to look at him. I got onion straws, I got desperation tips, I'm done with obligations. "Broke what?"

"My thing."

So of course the image flashes of Idras Melba holding his thing. GODS DAMMIT. But I know he's not standing behind me with his bruv in his hand. I talked to him about that before. I have no choice but to look up. I keep a bony tip in hand to fling just in case.

"My mojo," he says. "My joie, fam. I was spinning—"

"Phat beats?"

"Phat beats," he says with a sniff. "Folks dancin', movin'...then the inner beat crashed."

"You tried too phat a beat."

"I tried too phat a beat." Then he's about to rattle off his play list. I hold up a hand to stop him. The hand is greasy but he abides.

"Never give it more power after the fact, man," I say.

"I need to put my thing in your mouth, fam. You always know what to say."

"Idras?"

"Fam?"

"Shut the fuck up." He's not going to leave me in peace. I don't even know how he got in the house in the first place. "Here's what we're gonna do: you're gonna go to the settee—"

"You don't have a settee."

"SIT ON THE FUCKING COUCH, MELBA. You're gonna sit there...and draw the first person at the club to come to your mind."

"Bruv, it was dark, there were so many—"

"I don't care if you draw big boobs."

He sits, pulls a pad and stylus from his satchel, and immediately draws.

"Hell're you doing with an iPad Pro?"

"Bruv, you're the cheapest luddite ever walked," he

says without looking up. "Renaissance man, right? Ask what I did today?" He ticks off by making checkmarks in the air with the stylus. "Mad love. Check. Mad driving. Check. Fucking-A sandwich. A deal to play another black elk—"

"From the rabbit movie?"

"Different black elk. Smashed it at tennis with Serena. And then, then," he says, waggling that stylus at me like it's the finger he usually waggles, "I turnt a frikking club up. All the way, bruv. Tom Jones, P-Funk, Woody Guthrie, Sara Bareilles…"

The fuk?

"…some Husker Dü for the—"

"I get it, Idras."

"…then I lost my thing. The thing that makes Idras Idras, y'know?"

"The joie de vivre."

"Naw, fam, just the joi. Vivre is on lock."

"And the person you're drawing?"

"Goddess, bruv."

"Looks like an 8 on its side from here."

"See, you're on the surface of things. Deeper, bruv, deeper. Get deep in me."

"I just want my rib tips, man."

"She come in in tank top and body paint, bruv. Reds and neon blues, green. Like the dopest space chick since Batgirl was on Trek, ya feel?"

I nod.

"You feelin me? Are you feeling me? How's your grip?"

"I'm...yeah. Double fisted, man."

"I watched her dance, fam. She weren't dancing with nobody. Music was the partner. She's moving and shaking and bouncing that big beautiful body-n-soul to every mix I can come up with. Bruv?"

"Yes, bruv?"

"Bruv?"

"Oui?"

"Bruvver...she made Hootie and the Blowfish sexy."

"Shut your lying mouth."

"Serious as the Queen's girdle, bruv. She *embodied* shit, bruv."

"Is that when your thing broke?"

"Yeah. Is that love, bruv?"

"Hell no, you creepy motherfucker, you were just watching somebody dance! What that is, is you were spinning with intention and she spiraled right the fuck through every last one of 'em like they weren't even there. She didn't need you, man. She didn't need the DJ."

He repeats this. "She didn't need the DJ."

"Naw, bruh. DJ needed her."

Idras sets the stylus on my settee. He looks at the figure 8 of boob.

"You feel like you need to know her name, don't you?" I say.

"Yeah. Yeah, I need to say thank you to her. You know the Stones song, *She's A Rainbow*?"

"Everywhere."

"She was everywhere, man! She was nowhere. I don't think she ever opened her eyes but she never bumped into a single person. Just swaying. Moving. Music like Braille to her. She saw the room, she saw the room…"

"But she never saw you."

"Naw," he says softly. He looks at me with those big sleepy eyes. "I was holdin' the music but she never saw me."

"Music don't belong on a tether, bruh. Repeat after me, Idras Melba: Nobody needs the DJ; the DJ needs them."

"Don't wanna."

I flick a bone tip at him. It lands on the settee. I like saying fucking settee. He looks at it.

"Get that greasy thing off my settee, fool!" I snap. He taps it onto the floor with the stylus.

"What I'm saying," I continue, "Is you thought you were the joie. Nah, son. On the receiving end you're the vivre; they're the joie. WE are the joie, right? You, me, as long as we're on the receiving end of beauty. You didn't break your thing, man, you grew it."

"Long, fat, proud, resplendent—"

"Dude, seriously?" Then I nod at the pad. "Put that away. You know what you gotta do: ask the goddess her name. Give thanks for the knowing of it. Wish her well."

"But it ain't love though?"

"Not the way you want it to be. Get the fuck up and go find her. Thank her."

He gets the fuck up. He moves in for a hug.

"Can't hug you, man, hands are greasy," I say. Sweater dude had on cost more than my entire wardrobe. I could respect that.

"I love you, bruv," he says.

I nod.

"Fam? I love you, fam."

"Ok."

He looks at me stupefied. "CAN I GET SOME FREAKING LOVE BACK, MAN?"

I just smile sadly. I give him the nod though, then say, "Idras?"

"Yeah?"

"If her name is Alice keep your natural ass out of my house."

He leaves.

I go back to my frikkin cold desperation rib tips, but by then I don't even want to put in the effort.

Idras got into me. Got in me deep.

I toss the tip on my plate and sigh.

I want to know her name too.

Sophia Da'ren

The plan was to travel back in time and piss off Señor Wences so much that he threw Topo Gigio at me. Screw up some serious timelines, right? Instead I wound up in Sophia Da'Ren's bedroom right before she normally wakes up.

Which she did.

I had 2 seconds before Sophia Da'Ren opened a can of whup ass that would shame my line for generations to come. What do you do?

You sing. I sang the only Italian I knew. "Nessun dorma…" I sounded like shit but Sophia thought this was something Marcello cooked up. Why else would a tall black dude be in her bedroom in December murdering one of opera's most respected pieces?

She scooched up, covers dangerously close to revealing gawd, and laughed at the wonder of friendship, saying, "Sing!"

All I know is that one line of the song. I make stuff up. "Nessun dorma, boot regalia" that kind of stuff. Then I hit the big finish with "Mi amore!" 'cause that's what it sounds like they're saying, if I recall correctly, "L'amore! LA AMORRRRRE!"

I've only got 60 seconds left before the timeshift slung me back to where I came from. Time and Space are absolute shit. You accidentally shift to Sophia Da'Ren's presence and you can't stay? What kind of universe is that?

60 seconds.

She's about to speak but I quickly pantomime silence. How to communicate that the universe created so few examples of perfection that it would be a shame not to protect her? How to say your performances taught me—as a boy, as a young man, as whatever I am now—that being contrary and passionate were often the sparks of life?

I take off my shirt.

Sophia raises an eyebrow.

I draw a circle around my heart. A green circle forms on the skin. A hatch opens. I'm a time-traveling cyborg, try to keep up. Most futures depend on it.

Sophia's not scared. More fascinated and intrigued than anything. I'm sure she's thinking Marcello went all-out this time.

The revealed mechanism is a matrix of light. If you stare at the light it coalesces. It is a mini-museum of beautiful things: sunlight, freshly-washed hair, Sophia Da'Ren's neck, a Mariachi band, and movies, so many movies, with key performances from her. She watches these snippets, and it naturally dawns on her that this is not Marcello. That this is the future. That I came back to show her she matters.

No point whatsoever letting her know my presence is an accident of me trying to set into motion a series of seemingly unrelated incidents designed to have Rosario Dawdur cross my path on October 27, 2022—in the flesh rather than in the virtual world in 2189--all beginning with Señor Wences throwing Topo Gigio at me live on *The Ed Sullivan Show*. It's best to let her have this moment; I've only got 15 seconds left.

I tap my chest plate. It closes quietly like those self-closing kitchen drawers. Light fades, fades more, light's gone. It's just me and her in the room, sun streaming in on both of us. She hugs her knees, bare shoulders cresting the covers, and right then I know that it was no accident me being here. Future-future me somehow engineered this. There was more good to be done by rippling time with a smile in the early morning than showing Señor Wences to have an unlikely temper.

"Bravo. Gracie," she says.

10 seconds left. I don't wanna freak her out by dissolving in front of her. I bow, retrieve my shirt, and back

out of the room, saying "Gracie, amore" just as I close the door and disappear. Maybe future-future-future me set something entirely different in motion.

Maybe there are no accidents.

But then I remember what Elijah McCoy told me just before the maiden voyage of his 18th century TARDIS. "Time's an accident," he said, "but sometimes it gets it right. Feel like traveling?"

Pam Dear

I'm minding my own business, cussing about Comcast—excuse moi, fucking Comcast—when I notice people shying away from me at the bus stop. Generally I don't care about people at bus stops unless they're kneeling praying. I feel that on a deep, emotional level. But the fact that even Crazy Eduardo leaned away from me made me look up from the bill in my hand—excuse, overdue bill that I wasn't gonna fucking pay because service had been out four times in a month, meaning the lackbastards owed me—and yes, Pam Dear was there—which would make anybody jump back for glory—but what she had in her hands was another story entirely.

Pam Dear had a bottle of Djinn.

I could tell from the way she held it that it wasn't any old Djinn bottle either. This was top shelf, ancient powers, cosmic oasis right at your fingertips Djinn, the bottle so fluid, so curved in interesting ways I didn't doubt Pam Dear was meant to hold it.

But then she held it out to me.

Crazy Eduardo dropped to his knees, genuflecting.

You know how you suddenly become a supercomputer

able to assess information across infinitely bisecting planes, all within two nanoseconds? One: I know I'm not worthy on several key points here, first being that's Pam Dear, second being I'm the kind of guy complaining about his Comcast bill at a bus stop, third but not final being that bottle.

That bottle is gorgeous, man.

Imagine mercury. Then drop a few drops of black ink in it. Now imagine you're telekinetic; you're swirling and slaloming the mercury without touching it, stretching it into ribbons that twist like water trying to maintain its balance. The silver-black gleams like a monolith from outer space, and considering that it houses a djinn, it may very well be. It catches light on one part of its body then flints it out somewhere else. It's like Christmas. A tree of caressed glass.

Pam's not saying a word.

I supercomputer-nod. It's all on me, whatever "all" is, whoever "me" am. I is. Doesn't matter if I sound like Bizarro. I need you to focus. I need you to understand. I need you ready. I need you to notice things.

One: the bottle doesn't have a top. There's no stopper, cork, or screw-off cap. It's an unbroken, seamless, magnificent sculpture containing power you might never ever get to see or use.

Two: Pam's holding it with her fingertips. It's not a decision, it's an offering. Do you know what to do when Paradise offers gifts? Do you know what to do when more beauty than you've ever seen in your life says hello? Might not even say it with a word. Might step up to you at a bus stop. Might expect you to take a bottle of Djinn carefully and reverently from her fingertips to yours. Might stay there watching you with a smile. Might smile even more when you consider for a moment, then you turn around and hold the bottle out toward Eduardo, who gets up—crying even more than when he was on his knees—and makes his fingertips an extension of his entire soul.

Pam Dear walks away, but she's moving slowly. I'm supposed to walk with her.

Fuck the bus. The sun is out and there's a trash can up ahead. Perfect for filing unnecessary things. I rip the Comcast bill in half, drop it in the trash, and intake the biggest sigh I've had in a long time. Air filling me up feels good. Feels like djinn smoke coiling inside my glass frame. Except I'm not made of glass. I'm warm to the touch. Which I'm glad for, as Pam Dear is beside me.

I exhale.

"There's a little bar down the road," she says. "You thirsty?"

"Yeah," I say, thirsty, hungry, maybe even horny in the way that's a servant's smile, not a king's leer. "Yeah," I say, looking past the traffic, even the concrete, at something deeper than anything I'd bothered to understand. "I could drink."

Notice things, ok? Keep an eye out for that bottle of Djinn.

The Dream Factory, Oh Ho!

"Hey, Idras, they wanna know if you wanna do *Cats*."

"That's sick, bruv, I'm not into pervo--"

"Dude, the play."

"A play about cats? Tot'ly missed that. Deep allegory, right, maybe a little Egyptian mythos in the cut?"

"No, just a bunch of grown ass people acting like cats."

"Like...lickin themselves and what?"

Nod.

"Come on, fam, stop shittin me."

"I'm not."

"Bruv. Bruv?" Pauses. Frowns. Almost reconciles it. Re-frowns. "Bruv?"

I wait.

"They wanna do a movie?"

Nod.

Idras sits heavily on the couch, butt at the cushion's very edge, elbows on thighs, hands dangling. Head dangling. Bruv speaks to the floor: "Why? What's the angle, yeah? What're we missing..."

Shit, shit, shit, he's going down the hole...

"Alice... What. Have. You. *Done*?"

"ALICE GOT NOTHING TO DO WITH CATS, IDRAS MELBA--well, actually, wait. Does seem like the diabolical heinousness she'd hit us with."

"So, what, they want me to roll around on the floor and whatnot?"

"That's pretty much the entire play sooo..."

"Googobs of money?"

"Lulumoms will raid the wine fund to see you roll around on the floor."

"I'm in."

"What?"

"Ha, joking with you, bruh! Pullin your willy!"

"What?"

"Bruv. The ONLY way they'll get me to do summing like that is if they get Dame Fooking Judi Bench! Tell 'em to call me then, ha!"

Deep sigh. I sit next to him. "Bruv," I say.

Regrets, I Have A Few

Idras opened his gift and immediately cried. It was a green button affixed to a box.

"Bruv...is this?"

I nodded. "Yes. A time machine. You can go back. You can fix this!"

He wiped his eyes, nodding as well.

"Make it right before things get worse," I said.

No hesitation, He pressed the button. In that moment an infinite number of hims appeared then winked out in a flash so bright I couldn't see for hours. If only that flash had occurred when he took me to the red carpet premiere of *CATS*. But if this worked I wouldn't remember a thing. We as a species wouldn't remember. We would rebuild. We would grow. We would turn away from such foolishness forever...

...if it worked.

No Isolation

"My navel hasn't had a proper dusting, bruv," says Idras. For once, I know what he's talking about. We're sitting by a lake. It's windy, clouds are heavy but they're the kind that hold on rather than release.

"All this," he says, waving a hand at the beautiful scene, "this is the shit, right, fam?"

I nod.

"Viruses and idiots, that ain't the shit. Bruv, do you know how many rolls of toilet paper the studio sent me?"

I do, 'cause I took some.

"And I'm wondering where I fit into this shit, y'know? How much of me do I need to subtract to get summing to make some sense?"

I don't say anything.

Both of us stare at the water a bit.

"You're pretty quiet," he says.

"Speaking to all the fam for a minute," I say.

"Telepathically?"

"Maybe."

"Folks don't sit 'n listen to water as much as they should, bruv. Clear those navels out."

"You're sexy as a philosopher, Idras Melba."

"I know."

The area reminds both our navels of fish and rain and dirt and grass touching feet. There's a brightness to the grey sky. It's still early morning so Idras takes off his shirt. I'm about to follow suit--

"Bruv, don't."

His abs shake their heads no at me too. They're gentle about it though.

"One day I'ma have an ab, Idras," I say.

"I know, fam," he humors.

"Not that that's important."

"Ain't important at all." He puts a muscled arm around my cushy shoulder. "Can I tell you what's important, what just now traveled from my butt to my brain faster than Johansson snapping up a role?"

"Hit me."

"The only time any of us on this planet are happy...is when we think we've done some good for someone else. Huh? Yeah? I'm acting, right, but that's 'cause somebody out there might need 90 minutes of rest from their fucking lives shitting on 'em. Stupid as it is, I love acting. I get to be weird and get paid for it."

"Yeah."

"Fucking PAID, bruv."

"Yes."

"Like, holy fuck, the ducats, son..."

I'm quiet again.

"You thinkin 'fuck yo couch' over there, ain't you?" says he.

"I am."

"That's why you're fam. You're goofy but you're honest. Know what, take off your shirt, bruv."

"I'm not really a shirt taker offer, Idras."

"Air out that navel! You think Mother Existence gives two shits about moobs and bellys? Mother Existence is all, 'Oy, free the tiddys!' We're the ones fucked about flesh. We are the world, dude. Bring 'em out, man, get some air on them nipples. Let me be the wind blowing across some tips."

I look at him. He looks at me. He's earnest af. "You're a fucking poet, Idras Melba." I pull off my shirt. Wind feels good. Makes me feel like I'm in motion even though I'm not.

"Navels, bruv," he says.

"Navels," I say. We lay back to watch the sky, hands laced behind heads, chests full of air, our navels gazing for a change without their views restricted.

It's nice.

A couple drops of sun might even fall in there.

The Q Continuum

Idras, having decided early on that pants and knickers during quarantine were detriments, gave no fuks during Zoom calls.

"Idras, come on, man, I've seen it enough!"

"Bruv, it's just a little meat, yeah? Unprocessed sausage. You see yours every day."

I shake my head. I'm so tired.

"Look me in the eye, bruv," he says.

"I'm trying."

"Look me in the eye."

"Dude…mute your dick."

"It's just me here and you there. Let's talk about our feelings. You're in quarantine—" he pauses to take a sip of Grey Goose from a glass so crystal I know it costs more than my health insurance—"I call it the Q Continuum, right, and you: you're filthy and poor. Explore that feeling, fam. Chin up, bruv." He crosses his legs, leans back, and rests his arms along the top of a brand new blue Buccololly couch, improving the view not one whit.

But he's patient. He waits me out. He's sincere.

I sigh, close my eyes, and think for a second.

"Something masochistic about humans," I say. "They got an appetite for pain like it's pizza."

"Like bein' a zombie is our evolutionary pinnacle," says he with a curt nod approving my assessment. He uncrosses his legs and leans forward, elbows now on knees, chin thoughtfully atop knuckles. It's all I can do to avoid hearing 'The vole emerges from its den' in Attenborough's voice. "Yeah, I know things are hard all around. What're you using for toilet paper, bruv, pelts?"

"Toilet paper."

"Use the entire squirrel, right? You should've stayed here with me, bruv. I got a grotto. Fuck's the US know about a grotto? How're you set for beats?"

"They're phat."

"Bumping?"

"Bumping."

"Good, good. Take off your pants, son."

"I'm good."

"Dude, bruv, fam: It's just you and me."

"And Topo Gigio over there."

"Don't name my dick, fam, that's weird."

"I just," I fumble for words, "I don't know. Bruh, when'd the world become the director's cut of *Human*

Centipede? Tr*mp, disease, racism, repeat; every damn day swallowing that down as breakfast. I'm here by myself; not using pelts as toilet paper, but I slowly cut a Cheeto with a knife yesterday and slowly, carefully speared it with a fork. THAT AIN'T LIFE, IDRAS. Crazy white people are carrying guns as long as fourth graders in public, which is a clear sign that they should not have said guns, saying fuck the COVID, disease is their right. The vice president is so closeted he wakes up in Narnia every day, yet during a pandemic he still finds time to push his anti-gay agenda. I haven't had a decent orgasm in 7 years—"

"Bruh, the epidemic's only been going on for 2, 3 months?"

"SHUT THE FUCK UP, IDRAS MELBA." I put my shame in my hands, breathing through my fingers for a couple heartbeats before showing him my entire haggard face again. "Fam. I'm tired."

He tosses a nod in the Zoom direction of my pants. "Take 'em off, bruv."

"Don't they keep an archive of Zoom chats?"

"Your peen's not historical. Nobody's gonna uncover it a hundred years from now."

"I'm keeping the underwear on."

Idras smiles knowingly. "No, you're not."

I stand.

I take off my pants.

I sit.

"How's it feeling?" says Idras.

I feel like a person in front of their computer in their unsexy underwear, which is so oddly constricting a feeling I immediately want to howl. I squirm, pretending to try to get comfortable. I'm not comfortable like this, though, am I? This half-exposed imitation of life. Not comfortable with human centipedes, Karen zombies, racist cops, grifter Presidents, #MILF trending on Mother's Day, a *Venom* sequel, my sister-in-law's fascination with *The Masked Singer*, hornets that shiv, or, or...

"Doesn't feel right," I say to him.

"You feel connected to pain, dunnit?"

I nod. I even look off to the side and keep nodding.

"Lose the knicks, bruv. It's just you and me. Trust."

Trust.

Trust that things improve. Evolution demands improvement. Evolving from emotionally & spiritually-constrained frightened child-people to open, truthful adults Zooming naked like Idras Melba and not giving 2 fucks about it.

I can do this.

I can join the Q Continuum.

The Idras Quarantine Continuum.

Off go the draws, but I kick the laptop over doing it.

"Bruv...you all right?" Definitely real concern in his voice.

I right the computer. "Dude...I'm naked."

"Hell yeah you are."

This might be the first time I've ever felt relaxed on a video call. Even my cheap tattered sofa feels softer under my ass. "You think Rosario does this?" I ask—then catch myself. But it's too late. The thought's out there. He and I sit with it a moment.

"I can add her to the call," he says, and quicker than I can protest, he disappears. I hear a cell conversation in the background, his part of it. I hear his heavy home-alone footsteps coming back.

"Fam, Rosario in 30 secs."

I've never died and resurrected so much in the span of a heartbeat as right then.

But I ride it out. Idras is chill. No panic in the Q Continuum. Just realness. Just honesty. Joy.

The name "Rosario" pops up in a square.

Then she's there on video, wearing but a wide, bright smile and her entire best life.

We talk for hours.

I Swear To Gods It's All True*

Casey Masum. You remember that name? Casey's on the phone. "Claybourne? Here are the top ten reasons I'm going to kick your ass," that being a little unsettling to hear in such clear, professionally-crisp yet astonishingly warm tones. I recover quickly enough to run mental inventory of recent transgressions against Man, deity, and deejay. Pretty sure I've wronged humanity in innumerable ways. Almost a given. God? Holy water burned me but I maintain it had algae in it; it's not like they change that water often. And the only time I have ever in my life disrespected a deejay— and I tell Mr. Masum this—was when I gave one a mixtape and asked him to use it.

"So it wasn't you telling Kevin Back Bacon to call me repeatedly requesting Mariah Carry's version of *Aquaboogie* for his Marine brother he hadn't seen since 1973 but knew no matter where he was…he was giving 110% of his heart?"

"Mathematically impossible."

"Did Casey Masum tell you to speak on his colloquials?"

"No, sir."

"Say it again."

"No, sir."

"And that, America, is how permission works."

"But I have never, NEVER, spoken to Kevin Back Bacon, Casey Masum."

"Did you speak it to anyone?"

"I might've muttered it while I was drugged out of my gills in the hospital. Nearly died, you know."

"Nurse?"

"Huh?"

"You had a nurse?"

"Yeah."

"She heard it."

"So?"

"There's no information on this planet that Kevin Back Bacon won't get access to, so you basically told the most powerful person in the world to make my life hell."

"That six degrees thing is a myth—"

"CASEY MASUM WILL KICK YOUR ASSCHEEKS SO HARD THEY TURN INTO CLAPPERS! There are legitimate people out there stalking high school crushes they haven't seen in ages via poignant power ballads, and you've got Kevin effing Back Bacon harassing me."

"Meningitis, Casey Masum. Brain was cooking itself to soup."

"Are you giving Casey Masum your Top Ten Excuses For Being A Pathetic Jackass?"

"No, sir, I just have one."

"Caller…"

"You called me, Casey Masum."

"Caller?" and then I hear the doorbell his way. Phone drops. Muffled voices. Then footsteps returning. The sound of angry breathing precedes his voice. "Claybourne from Detroit? I just received a registered letter from, you guessed it, Kevin Back Bacon. 'Dear Mr. Masum, My name is Kevin. When my baby brother was 12 he was sent to the marines. Five years later, I was born. (America, this is the kind of shit Kevin Back Bacon plays.) He and I would trade letters with *Aquaboogie* lyrics as our own special code. 'Never learned to swim' was him saying indoctrinated aggression really didn't sit well with him. 'Can't comprehend all the strokes' was pubescent me admitting that sex truly baffled me. Well, by the time he and I became twins, a lot had passed: Reagan, America's fascination with chimps in buddy vehicles, '80s hair, and, yes, any notion of peace the world ever held. My brother's tour got extended 37 times. In all his travels around the world, somehow we lost touch. But I'll never forget the last message he sent me: 'Go 'head wit yo funk, underwater boogie baby.' So, Casey, for my brother who's somewhere dressed in face paint and fatigues with his sights currently on target to release freedom from his gun, can you play Mariah Carry's Christmas album version of *Aquaboogie* in the hopes that unnecessary octave changes can bring the lost finally and permanently back together?'"

Then phone goes quiet an extra second more than it should have.

"I'm not a joke," says Casey Masum.

"You're the voice that brings thousands together," I say.

Quiet phone.

"Casey?"

"Does Kevin Back Bacon even have a brother?"

"Who knows? Who cares? Hell, we're all Kevin's kin. Including you."

"Kevin loves me somewhere out there?"

"Somebody that hates you ain't trying to make you laugh at the piquant ridiculousness of life."

Phone goes quiet again. A few seconds later: music on

his end. Volume increases.

Purple Rain.

"Claybourne from Detroit, this one's for you. Thank you." It's not just any version of *Purple Rain*, it's a live, extended version nobody's heard since the day it was performed in concert. It's got guitar interludes that give space for crying, drum riffs that uplift, and periods of silence save for one note held as precious as love itself. Casey doesn't say anything, just lets me listen all the way through. 17 minutes of bliss, uncut, commercial free, a Top Ten encapsulated into One. I didn't know Casey Masum doubted himself. I suppose everyone has pain.

"Casey…thank you. Damn and yes, thank you. How'd you get my number?"

"Maybe I'm Kevin Back Bacon," he says.

"Are you?"

"Only Kevin Back Bacon knows who's Kevin Back Bacon."

"You think he's lonely? Should we send him a song?"

"Tell you what, send a request to the show. If it reaches me, I'll see if I can get it on."

"Footloose?" I ask.

"Footloose," Masum agrees, and I can hear him

smirking.

"You cold as fuck, Casey," I say.

I wait. It's quiet over there. I wait some more. Then I realize Casey's hung up.

I think about blocking his number, but nah. He might want to call me back one day. I'm cool with that.

In memory of one of the greats

The Fall of It All

He hadn't called me "bruv" all day. I tapped the table, caught his eye, and across that bistro table asked, "The fuck, Idras?" as tenderly as I could.

He launched right into it. "You ever want summing so bad that when you get it you have no idea what it is? Like, your want warped it, y'know, and when you get the real you're like, fuck is this?"

"Er' day, Idras Melba. Er' day."

"Why is that, fam? What's the point of wanting shit if our cognitive abilities just piss it up?"

The waiter brought my tea and whatever cockney bullshit Idras was drinking. It was chilly out. Viola Mavis had burned all our sweaters. She had cause. I wrapped the cup in both hands, savoring the warmth and partaking of the steam. Idras poured extra whiskey from a silver flask into his cockney bullshit.

We waited a moment to see where our thoughts would go.

"This been locked and loaded in you for a while, eh?" I asked.

"See, I wanted Alice for a bit, bruv. Like deep in the

follicles, right? But then we spend a weekend together and it turns into a thing."

Idras and Alice had spent a weekend hunting down petrol executives. Office fires, poisoning. A Kodiak bear. Made the international news.

"Alice is certifiable," I said. "She tried to kill me with a tsetse fly and a felt hat."

"Nah, that was just trynta get you to loosen up." Idras heaved a deep sigh, squinted at the horizon over my shoulder, held the squint, held it, held it—"Am I the mum in that Preence song, bruv? Never satisfied?"

"You're not a Preence song, Melba."

"You know I'm a dove, bruv."

"Shut the fuck up. Ok, listen: Humans want shit, right? I want shit, all the way from sweet ass to a soaker tub that dispenses butter pecan cups. But I don't lock that in. Wants and desires need to flow, fam; gotta be loose sphincter with 'em, not tight. You loose?"

"I thought I was," he said, then admitted, "Not wide open like you. You could engulf the Statue of Liberty."

"Don't compliment me."

He stared at me with Idras intensity. "You're a wide open ass, bruv."

"Thank you?"

"You're damn right thank you. How'd you get to be such an asshole?"

"Dude…"

"I want…so much…to write a poem right now, y'know? Summing so tangible it makes ya weep, right? I want to connect, bruv. I wanna close my eyes and touch somebody and immediately know who they are."

"You know what I want? I want a bath, a two seater."

"You and me?"

"No, Idras."

He shrugged.

"I want to sit in a tub with somebody until we get wrinkly…and we're so warm we're rubbery… and there's laughing and drowsing and tiny questions of 'More hot water?' Maybe a little humming."

"A simple, wide open ass."

I sipped my tea. It was good. Hibiscus with a hint of ginger. No sugar. Just water and bagged bits. Water and bits in a cup. "My ass floats on a river of wants, Idras," I said, smiling at him in what I hoped was beguiling Yoda fashion. He leaned close to me.

"You holdin' one in, bruv?"

"Huh?"

"A fart."

"GODS DAMMIT I'M BEGUILING YOU!" It was hard shout-whispering that but I did it.

"But that means charmingly deceptive, fam--"

"Don't call me a wide open ass again."

--"You're a wide open ass."

"What do you want the most right now, Idras?"

"The most?"

"Yeah."

"I want a burger, bruv. Cooked by someone who loves me."

The waiter came back. He gathered a few messy bits off our tiny table. Just before he hurried away I stopped him with a hand on his forearm. "Excuse me," I said. I smiled at him. He smiled back. He reminded me of a young Steve Buscemi. I looked at his name tag. It was...

Donnie.

Oh hell yeah.

"Could we get 2 burgers? Medium well."

"Right. Back in 2 chops," he said. "I'll put chips on the side, yeah, courtesy of the house." He gave a nodding wink to Idras. I tended to forget Idras was a star. Then he disappeared into the coziness of the establishment of his employ.

"Free chips, Idras," I said.

His eyes brimmed a bit. "Bruv…you buying me a burger? You love me, brah?"

"I guess I love you, Idras. I guess I do."

"You feelin' dessert?" he said.

"Always."

"It's on me."

Nutbutter

"Bruv?"

"Where you going with this Idras?"

"You haven't even let me talk! Bruv? How're you on nutbutter?"

I sit up, cover my entire face with my hands and breathe into them for a bit.

"OK, Id, hit me."

"Just thinking about life, fam. Kinda strange how things are these little vortexes, right? And everything, like your opinions, your beliefs, the shit you do every day, is these wee, tight wind-devils."

"Can I interrupt?"

"Yeah."

"We're on a beach."

"Yeah."

"You know I had my hands behind my head, all of this," I draw a frantic circle to indicate my body, "on a lounge chair, right? Daydreaming my natural ass off."

"They're trying to turn us into gifs, bruv. All of us locked into repeating the same damn thing every interaction we think we're doing. Little repetitive bubbles of existence."

"What about my dreams?"

"You were dreaming about somebody naked, weren't you, bruv?"

Busted.

"Who was it this time?" he asks. "No, I don't even wanna know. Some gorgeous woman with pert nips and a desire to watch Harryhausen movies with you."

"All nips are pert nips," I say.

"Don't try political end runs on me, bruv. The daydream was about to end with you sitting there alone as fuck watching her walk away, wasnit?"

"Get outta my head, bro."

"Same moment, bruv! Same responses to stimuli. Beach. Sun. Nudity. If I gave you 3 headlines: outrage, disgust, frustration. Show you Dolly Parton: heart emoji. Discuss the phatness of my own beats: eyeroll emoji."

"I don't wanna hear about your phat beats," I mumble.

"Whassat?" he eggs, "whassat, bruv, right here, right here in me ear."

"Don't wanna hear about your phat beats, Melba!"

"You. Cut. Me. To the. Quick, son." Then he considers his larger argument a moment. "Know how people get in a rut?"

"Yeah."

"Well, this ain't like that. You can see when you're in a rut. Gif, though, don't know that it's stuck in gif. Gif's a trapped soul in a repeating moment till the stars burn out. It cannot change that, eh? Gifs don't fucking evolve, bruh. A rut's just that things have jelled up a bit, right? Jelly. Slow and sticky. Gif, though, that's peanut butter, bruh. Y'plopped right into the center of it."

"Don't pun me, Idras."

"Bruv, lemme finish."

"I see where you're going. Don't you do this."

"Bruv? I love you, bruv, and that's why I gotta let you know that the next person you feel a pull to say hi to, you say hi. Break the looped dream. All right? You promise me that? You promise me you're gonna analyze the moments and break the circuit before the loop closes?"

"Don't do it—"

"Bruv...choosy bruvvers don't choose gif."

Didn't he lay his ass back down, sip his drink, and close his eyes?

The next time I vacation with Idras, I'm getting a yurt. Separate. With a good lock. Never done a yurt before. I could run around naked in there all I wanted and it'd still feel like I was on a beach.

New ways. New things.

I look at Idras before I descend back to my daydream. Sun's full on his face. He's grinning like he sees me, sees that I'm looking at him, sees that in that look I'm agreeing with him, and in agreeing with him, sees he's won.

Choosy bruvvers don't choose gif.

Dammit, Idras.

I close my eyes, automatically hoping for a different dream.

Idras Coup

"I know you're in there, fam, I can see your nipple."

"Get away from my keyhole, Melba."

He goes quiet. I don't move. My yurt's leaf-shaped fan blades turn and turn.

"I need to talk about your country, bruv. You gonna keep sticking sparklers in squirrels' butts and whatnot?"

"THE HELL, MAN!"

I spill ungainly from my hammock, sprawl to the door, and fling it open.

"See, here's what I don't get," he says, ignoring my ire, "the orange guy. You know he's an idiot. He's been an idiot his whole life. A proper pig. It's not a secret, bruv."

"Do we haveta talk about this while I'm naked in a yurt?"

"You're nake' on a beach now. Might wanna…"

I run inside. Door's not locked. Idras follows.

"I almost saw an ab, bruv."

"Dude, why're we talking about this on my vacation?"

"No vacation from stupid, bruv. 4 years. You let 'im fuck up for 4 years. That's a whole term, bruh."

I got nothing to say.

"So question is, why does Murica hate itself so?" He sits on a wicker chair, crosses his legs, steeples his fingers, and waits.

I wrap myself toga-style in the gauzy sandy-colored sheet and pace, knowing he's not going anywhere.

Why does America hate itself?

"See, anybody constantly preening in a mirror got problems with 'emselves. Self-esteem's in the shit. You guys can't go 10 minutes without blessing your country, making sure the flag is wavin', or reminding yourselves that you're American...and you don't even know what fucking 'American' means! Give me one reason, bruv, why I shouldn't shitcan the lot of you."

"Is Idras Melba," I say to make sure I got this right, "is Idras Melba planning a coup?"

"I'm too sexy for politics, bruv."

This is true.

"Why don't you do it?" he says. "You know that petulant fuck only ran 'cuz he got fired from that TV show. Got angry as fuck, needed to rage wank, and Putin's like, hey fucklack, c'mere."

"Can I ask you a question? What time is it?"

"I 'unno. Six, seven ayem."

"WHY IN SEVERAL FUCKS ARE WE TALKING ABOUT THIS?"

"Because, bruv, the world's set to become a global fam, and your country's grown into the biggest cockup around. I need to put y'all on the counselor's couch."

"Dude…"

"Fam…yer country's got shitty little brother syndrome."

This stops my pacing.

"Right?" he says. "Like, all seething jealous of big brother—that's us."

"Britain fucking sucks, dude."

"I know. But psychologically, yuh've been in a snit 'cause Chad got the beemer 2 years before you."

"Fucking Chads."

"Fucking Chads. So you bake in all this bullshit hatery and furious ego masturbation, leading to hundreds of years later, this motherfucker thinking he deserves a second shit on everybody and—spoiler, bruv—a bunch of wonked fucks who agree with him! Y'all are individually-wrapped Brexits a billion times over."

What do I say to this? I'm in a toga. That Rome never died? That maybe there was too much lead in early

European kitchenware and mofos just ain't right? That for some reason psychosis sounds like a bitchin' band to follow to USians? What do I say to a country wrapped in a bunch of gauzy lies with their dicks clearly visible and woefully unimpressive?

Do I say I'll run for president?

Nah. But President Ocasio-Cortez has the ring of hallelujah to it. But that's for future times that can handle all'a that.

Right-now times need Viola Mavis in Boudica armor on a giant fucking horse, swinging a flaming mace at teeny mofos who think flag lapel pins and bullets get them the beemer before anyone else.

Fuck their beemer needs.

I can see Viola's campaign slogan: *'Fuck Is Wrong With Y'all?'*

Yeah.

Put the entire country on a national Buccololly couch. Treat European lead poisoning, prevailing small dick energy, racism masking self-hatred, and finally deal with beemer envy. President Viola Mavis taking her wig off just after the click of congressional doors locking freezes dumbfucks in their seats. No more shitting the bed for attention, America.

Time to yurt the fuck up and come correct.

Idras is smiling. Smiling that *You Should Be A Part Of The Solution* meme smile under sexy eyes plus the *afterward we fuck* impeccably-tailored suit, which he's not wearing (wearing an open shirt, neon green trunks, and scruffy flip-flops), but honestly when is Idras not an afterward-we-fuck meme?

Maybe we make that a campaign theme? *Get Your Shit Together; Afterward We Fuck*

It may not be politically astute, but I mean, hell, love is all we need.

"Maybe we can get the country to truly love itself for what it ought to be, huh?" I say.

"Shouldn't be that hard. All fucking wankers anyway."

Self-love 2020: You're All Fucking Wankers Anyway. Sold.

Distanced-Self Sex Ed with Idras

"You know who I wanna do when this is all over, fam?"

"Dude...we talked about this. You gotta leave that Charlize hunger be."

"No, no, naw," he says, dismissing that fantasy as so J'Adore ago. "Me. Myself, bruv. I'd be all over that."

I'm a little quiet.

"Think on it, bruv: who knows your body like you do? Not just TSA agent in the valley of Gwangi, but, like, y'know, those spots a bloke wishes somebody would find without telling 'em, right? Who knows *you*?"

"You wanted me to think you meant solely sexually, didn't you?" I say to the cagey bastard.

He touches a finger to the side of his nose. "You're learning me, bruv. Schoolin'. Professor. Who you wanna do?"

Of anybody? Including myself? Who and how do I wanna be touched when this quarantine is over?

"I want my hand up a Muppet," I say.

Idras blanches.

"Not like that, muthaflumper! I wanna do puppetry when this is over. I wanna feel like I can create life in 3 dimensions in case real life gets reduced again to 2."

Idras nods, the space between his eyes in full Klingon wrinkle.

"I want," I continue, "to do something that makes someone else laugh."

"Make 'em feel good, yeah?" he says.

"Yeah."

"Like phat beats."

"Your phat beats make people dance. What's better than dancing?"

"Hell yeah they do. So you wanna slam phat beats in a Muppet?"

"If I'm arrested, I'm blaming the fuk out of you."

"Seriously, bruv. Beats is all about the heart, right. You want your heart in summing."

He actually gets it.

He pauses sewing his Halloween costume, gets pensive for a second, then points that finger at me. "They say puppets are like familiars, bruv. Who'd you be?"

"Y'mean, like, a real Muppet? Like Fozzie or something?"

"You're no Fozzie."

"I could be Fozzie."

"Fozzie wuz happy naked with just a necktie and a hat. No ego."

"And no real talent."

"Spot on, that is f'you, agreed."

"Shut the fuck up, Idras Melba."

"No way you Gonzo. Gonzo's sex personified."

He goes back to sewing, and I immediately say, "Kermit."

"Kermit was lonely as fuck. You got me with you. I'm always here," he says.

"I'm not sure how you get in."

He ties off a final hold-knot and gnaws off the leftover thread. I have no idea what he's making. It's green and brown like a shag carpet got hella nauseous. "You ain't lonely, fam. Naw. Got too much love in you to be lonely. What you *are*..." his voice soars a bit and hangs ten... "is out of touch with summing important. It's like your Johnson's in your hand but you got no idea what to do with it."

"Oh my god..."

"Everybody wants to be Kermit cuz 'e's safe.

Everybody wants to be Animal cuz 'e's pure id. Responsibility on the one hand, passion on the other."

"So who am I, Idras?"

"You fucking Beaker motherfucker; running around on fire and not knowing why. Everybody's Beaker. We're all Beaker."

That hit me in the cut.

"People running around in Beaker suits 24/7," he says, "hoping to hell to act like they got shit together. Dude, you got Johnny Rocket wearing 'is strap-on munitions dick to Costco just in case the race war hits while 'e's getting' a tub o' cheese. Shit is not together."

"No. No it is not."

"Folks don't know who they wanna be. Who they wanna do. They need to fucking sit down and learn to sew."

"That might not be a bad idea."

"That's a damn good idea."

"Sew my soul into a puppet and let it be freer than me."

"Couldn't be any worse than the meatsuit you're in, right?"

"My meatsuit misses hugs, dude," I admit.

"Yeah, I know."

"Misses seeing people surprise themselves learning

things."

"Misses hoping to somehow rescue Rosario after she's fallen into a vat of baby oil."

"So much."

"Well, fam, if wishes were horses we'd all be kicked inna head."

"You already had the answer to your question, didn't you?" I ask.

"Never really a question."

"What're you sewing up?" I have to know. He's reaching into his sewing kit for a spool of differently-colored thread.

"Fermit"

"Dafuq?"

"Exactly. You're catchin' on, bruv."

"You're sewing Fermit Dafuq?"

"Only costume for me. Kermit and Fozzie. Fucking zen together. The only way to do the question of how to do me. 'Fuck are you, Idras?' I'm Kermit and Fozzie all in whatever fucks anybody's got to give toward questioning the freedom of me."

"So that's what you're gonna do when this is over, eh? Walk around in your Fermit suit?"

He rests his hands in his lap and regards me patiently. "Do *you* want a Fermit suit?"

"Course not."

"I can make the inner lining ribbed for your pleasure."

"Dammit…"

"Fam?"

"Yeah?"

"Bruvver?"

"Yeah?"

"Guv?"

I draw a deep breath.

"Responsibility and compassion coupled with no ego," he dangles. "How you wanna be done?"

"Fermit me," I say quietly.

He smiles, hand already moving for another pile of greenish-brown shag.

Don't know where he got that ugly-ass material…but it fucking works. He's got me.

"Shag me," I say. "Shag me good."

"Like there's any other way."

En Fin

"You ever wonder about the tips of things, bruv?"

"I'm not liking where this is going, fam."

"Think about it. Nips. We like 'em 'cause they're tips. Rib tips. Q-tips. Tip top. We're all about standing on tippy toe."

"Jumping off points."

"Yeah, but where we going to? Y'know? We jump thinking jumping's the whole show. Where we going, bruv?"

"I'm just trynta enjoy my shrimp," I say.

"Even shrimp, fam! What're that all over your plate? Shrimp tips! Why you afraid of the shrimp tip, son? Get that tip!"

"I don't want the tip, Idras."

"Get that tip in you!" He grabs a handful of my tips. "THIS...means something. Predilections, fears. Either we run toward the tip, or we slink away."

"I don't think you're supposed to eat the—"

"TODAY WE ARE CANCELING THE APOCATIPS!"

"Dude..."

"I usedta wonder where I'd wind up, y'know, as a kid? Had no idea I'd be naked on Zoom so much with you or slamming beats in penthouses."

"Phat beatz."

"Phat beatz. I was at the base of everything. Poor and filthy like you."

I stare at him, shrimp half in my mouth.

"I don't think I ever even looked up, bruv, to see the tips. Everything was just base."

"You were basic af."

A shrimp tail zinged with force and accuracy hurts. Hit me right in my third eye.

"Now that I'm at the tip, I can jump higher. Thing, though, about that is: you never see where you're going. Jump down, always a view. Jump up from tip? You don't know what's up there!"

"Act of faith?"

"No it's not an act of faith 'cuz you already know it's gonna be sweet, you're on the tip, man! What you don't know…is how even *more* tip is gonna change you."

"Like nothing spoils like success?"

"Like nothing's more terrifying than knowing circumstances *do* change your guts, yeah? Is why we like tips…but only up to a certain point. I think we should worship the tips, bruv. Gonna start worshipping mine."

"You know it's hard for me to look you in the face, right?"

"A nip when it's flat and warm is safe. A nip when it's cold and poinked? Dangjuh! Erect nipples are like meteors falling out of the sky, bruv, toppling society and shit."

"So we gonna cancel the nipple apocalypse?"

"Right frucking today, luv." He gets up, heads for the kitchen. "Take your shirt off," he calls back.

"Why?"

"I'm getting some ice."

So I've got a few seconds to wonder: do I let Idras Melba ice my nipples to lead me to epiphany, or do I sit there with my shirt on, sit there hastily finishing my shrimp, remain in place resigned to simultaneously loving and fearing the tips of all things in a society that says strive but never actually knowing for what?

Is a few seconds time for me to figure that shit out?

I take off my shirt.